House of Ecstasy

Kala Joy

"My joy is the joy of eternity, and my laughter is the drunken laughter of a harlot in the house of ecstasy." Book of Babalon

For Jack Parsons

Serpent coil up around me through me I am ready to feel again I am ready for passion to rise within me I am ready for all you have to offer I am ready to approach the world again with newness of trust born of my innocence of my joy that is pure that is the way I came into the world that is the way I am in the world that is the way I move out of the world that is the way I will come back into the world.

Ouroboros

She willed her lips to kiss,
and the kiss poured like water
down his chest, sent light
up his spine, danced with his
inner spiral.

He gasped with each lavish
lick up his perineum
to the tip of his penis.

Her mouth wet and warm
held him while he kissed
forever her belly, her hips
then drank from her spring.

Together one serpent
mouth open wide

orbits infinity—

gush
    gush

 gush

and

        swallow.

Swallow

The birds sing Spring into being.
Brown beaks peck at the snow,
reveal tiny seed.

They sing to their loves,
throats wide and free.

They make love as World listens.
Branches swoon to touch them.

Them

I never thought I'd be like them.
Spread wide before the lens,
offer my body as a banner
to pleasure, wave it high,
allow love shudders to flutter
and the wind to carry the message
sex is beautiful.

    sex is beautiful

Yet here I am, naked in the arms of my lover.
The camera trembles in the hands of another—
spectators hearing of the show, line up to see

me wear ecstasy like a Queen's crown,
wave my scepter from the float.

In the streets, the people tear off their clothes,
finger paint each other's bodies
bright as colored eggs.

Rainbows stretch out over the boulevard
for the Easter parade.

Parade

At the end of flags waving,
confetti littered the street
where a silver crown lay flattened.

A single clown remains.

Naked, his wig disheveled under his arm,
he remembers how her throat let loose
moans that snapped his suspenders.
How he groaned as he came
watching her come.

The Fool now alone
in the manner of kings
rises from the curb,
reaches for the star.

Star

She shined that way from the center of the circle.
Her lake of light lapped the shoreline.
The people stood on her edges,
gaped at her shimmer and glitter,
and needing her touch, jumping into her water,
burned themselves to ashes.

Ashes

The city burned.

From the destruction leapt green things.
Sprouts from seed that had waited so long
for calamity, now celebrated in the rubble.
Grasses grew up where the asphalt buckled,
cracks became luminous streams to feed new
populations. The sun overhead gleamed.
Bright ones pushed aside concrete and brick,
stretched out their wings and sang a new
world into being.

The city reflected in the star's gaze
the House of Ecstasy.

Ecstasy

On the park bench they kiss for all to see.
On the roadside, lovers fall into each other.
On the rooftop, she stands naked, invites the rain.
On her body, lovers come and go, all are welcome.
On the lawn, hundreds of bare bodies
sit, lay, eat, write, play guitar, do yoga, laugh, sing,
grow, dance, paint, cry, fuck and find each other.

Other

When other is me
I am free.

Free

Everything about me sacred,
I open wide and spray my sea
clear to the sky and higher.

We lay in the warm wet of me
all night long.

Long

There are times for short and sweet.
Then there are times to linger
long and lush until dawn.

Both ways can be found here
in this house, both ways
to ecstasy embellished
on the tip of my tongue.

Today, we'll take the scenic route.

Envision the place as round,
altars surround you;
Aphrodite basks in amethyst glow.

In the center on soft cushions, you wear
under garments of flowers and dew.

The sound of waterfall gushes
from a balcony over your head.

Lover with his fingers and eyes
caresses your cheek to arouse
the divine murmur,
the yes that invites him
down

staircases
into scarlet and purple
interiors.

He explores every crevice,
every cupboard
that beckons, every
door that holds a secret.

You invite him deeper
into places unknown
even to yourself
until this moment.

Together you descend—
twin ribbons unravel
from your hair
and over the banister.

The two of you
risk all, hold ribbons,
leap midair
and slide down spiraling.

The ascension happens
all at once;
you levitate, shine,
shoot up through the roof
to stars.

Colors twirl and dart,
wings flap and flip,
higher and higher
until floating
on a wish

you come
down.

Down

Needle and thread, we push into dream,
stitch thrice the seam.

Seam

A quite talented seamstress,
her creations worn by dancing
girls and tantrikas,

she covered them in silk and beads,
dangled jewels from their earlobes
while stealing kisses.

For herself, she wore only pale pink
gauze, tied with a crimson sash.

Sash

Once a belly dancer with purple eyelashes
tied the seamstress to the street sign with her own sash.

Then she danced before her, offering
her to men that passed
who could see bare flesh through
the gauze and who brought gifts.

The bright boy who sang her a song
took her home.

Home

Women and men lounge on couches.
Oil scents the air ylang ylang,
rose, jasmine, musk.
Lace and silk robes
decorate the doorways,
arms thin and full
beckon.

Men and women come
holding roses, perfume,
the finest tea and incense.
They place their gifts on the altar
and wait.

Women speak in whispers
kiss each other in corners.

Men hug on the stairway.

Women and men meet on cushions
where everything is permitted.

In this place of every pleasure
I live.

Live

Plates of fruit and leaf that hold the sun.

We fill our bellies with live food,
let light fill our cells,
let the colors of the rainbow
make our skin glow
like children again.

Our house fills with vitality.
Our dreams fill the rooms.
Our ecstasy fills the planet.

The planet filled with our joy
blooms.

Blooms

Under the snow, seed awaits bloom.
The sun wears an orange robe,
billows over the sky
for the lover horizon
who pulls him down to her bed.
.

When the darkness comes
they crawl beneath dark blankets
in the afterglow of the day.

Quickening, quivering under soil
beneath snow, their child
awaits the dawn's red glow.

Glow

Their faces glow like fireflies at sunset
when they emerge from the yurt.

He goes to pick up his son from school
while she gathers wood for the evening fire.

There are dishes to put away
and laundry dries in the sun.

She dreams a kale salad
with hemp seeds

while she practices
belly dance

and reaches for the words
to describe

the blue light that glowed
on her third eye as she came,

the mist she saw move
across the floor,

the jaguar that rose up in her belly
and kissed the serpent,

the munay that came
when his blue eyes

melted like
icicles,

dripped into
her mouth.

Mouth

Then he
showed me
how very
much
he loved
to kiss me
there.

There

You whispered Shakespeare in the temple
before making love for the first time.

Thou art more lovely

Let's talk about what happened
there on that floor, we the babes who
the universe implored.

How did it feel for you
when I spiraled to maelstrom
so every one there fell into me

and you had to leave the room
reeling away from my laughter?

Sometimes too hot the eye of heaven shines

Did you realize I was high
on your breath

and that when She came into me
She came because of you?

And this gives life to thee.

Thee

At night the Lady dropped a bed sheet rope
over the balcony and let herself down
to the street.

Her lips painted red, her hair to her knees,
her bosom pushed up like buttocks on her chest.

She stood on the curb by the horses
and lifted her skirt

to the gentleman in the carriage
who opened the door

let her in

gave her sweets to suck
noticed the pale softness
of her hands

but never said a word
about her secret.

Later, before the iron gate of her estate
his horses stopped.

She hid her eyes.

Still silent, he handed her
his card.

Card

The house throws flames
at the streetlight.
Inside, the cat
cowers behind the door,
breathing black air.

She scries in the toxic
clouds a past
that courted ashes.

An image of herself
rises in the sky—
naked, dripping
candle wax
on her breasts
while her lovers
gasped.

Who in the crowd
can imagine
what is being
offered now
to the fire?

The insurance man
before her smiles.
She thinks perhaps
he may know
what debauchery
burning looks like.

In her palm his card
wilts and bends.

Call if you need anything.

Anything

Everything is permitted,
she told him.

Anything you desire
dances into being
before your wonder.

The last time she saw him,
he ran his fingers over
his chemo bald head.
His eyes flirting with death,
shimmered.

Now he flirts with her
as she lays upon
his table; he works the kinks
out of her shoulders.

He knows now the value
of going for what he wants.

His eyes take a dive
into her liberty.

His hand roves
over her bum.

Later, after she leaves, he moves
through time and space
to visit her in bed.

31

They celebrate; his spectral hands glow
with another sunset.

The throbbing at the center of her forehead
deepens when he gets inside her.

The ecstasy worth the pain,
she opens wider
her door.

Door

The door must be shut now
from his gaze, his fear
of girls kissing,
his difficulty
with the intimacy
of women.

Everything within balks
at this departure, this
partition he creates
to keep the river
from touching the sea.

You promise you won't let him
come between us.

The sunset glows
brilliant vermilion
as day light disappears
behind the mountain
and is gone.

Gone

This morning snow covered just there.
By afternoon, the Earth, startled by the Sun,
can no longer hide from him her body
beneath the white shroud of winter,
so lays back, wetter by the moment,
and enjoys his cyclopean gaze.

.

Small stones swim in puddles
that she sucks in to feed the seed.
Her body softens, expands,
allows green legs to kick
their way into flower—

out of darkness and into sight.

Sight

Outta' sight!
They said the year I was born.
My mother dressed somewhere between
mini skirts and maxi, her bee hive wig
pinned to her scalp with pins.
I buzzed around her dressing table,
my finger pads painted green, blue
eye shadow, salmon blusher, flower pink
lip stick like a push-up melted down
in its golden tube.
My face streaked with colors,
she called me 'little Indian' not
the glamour girl I saw in the mirror.
I wore her size eight honey colored pumps
down the stairs, silent when the ankle twist
sent me reeling into the front door.
I learned to keep the pain to myself
not risk experience cut down before it started,
avoid the even greater risk of her being right.
You'll twist your ankle!
She warned over and over
as I fell over and over down those stairs,
the pain that would make my mouth pretender
kept outta' sight.

Sight

The right men make passes
at girls who wear glasses

Glasses

After the divorce
she took out the special glasses
the crystal bells with silver rim
overflowing with red wine
for lover's kisses
even though it wasn't
Sunday.

Sun Day

Before pen meets paper,
she looks up, sees him
again for the first time.

Each ray an arrow...fly, fly, coming.

> Cupid giggles;
> his baby fat thighs
> hide behind cloud.

Her body shot through,
she falls on her back in the snow.
She watches

> thighs grow meaty,
> the cloud become loin cloth
> for Eros.

Reeking radiance,
he lifts her from the white
unlined page.

Blood leaks from her wounds,
drizzles into pattern,
seeps to feed the first shoot;

she becomes that shoot...
push, push her green
way to the surface.

She caresses her lover's bright face
with her finger.

Finger

Slip a finger in.

Let it sit and ponder
the feeling of wet
warm delicacy.

Let it wiggle
inspire giggles.

Let it dance in the pink
folds of her deepest secret.

Let it move to her music
slow and slower
and in between enjoy
letting light stream
from its tip into her core.

Let it quiver with tropical
adventure and melt
 into her rainforest.

Let it explore deeper
darker to the button hole
and slide back out
free form on water fall.

Let it spiral toward
and away from
her center

40

hold her with an arc
as she pours, spills
lets herself gush
over and down

the hand of God.

God

I only give it away for free.
My Word a world
I offer.

I ask only
that when my first flower
peeks up through the snow
to greet you

that you answer me
with warm kisses blown
over each fragile petal.

I ask only
that you give it
all away.

Away

I went away.

You looked for me
in my room.

I wasn't there.

Not hopping under the bed
with the bunnies.

Not curling myself into a hat
in the hatbox.

Not flattened into wallpaper
watching you pace the floor.

Not the apple for your teeth.
Not the wire leading to your computer.

Finally you caught a glimpse
when outside in the night,
you saw my miraculous light spiral
from deep in the forest.

You knew then I went away,
and dropping your skin by the door,
you followed.

Followed

I followed your alien
Underworld singing, music enticing,
lyrics dancing like a white scarf tied to a black
hat worn by you as you ran ahead of me,
teasing out my comprehension just as you slipped
into a sudden hole in the leaf bed.

I knew then how some day I would know you
and learn how to stalk the branches,
searching like you for bright berry melodies
that beg for a taste of tongue.

So many hours I sat by this hole,
waiting for the tip top of your hat
to peek through, your blue eyes
clearing a path through me;
with a glance sending me into the sky
high enough to wear the pie shaped cloud—
you and me painted the colors of sunset,
captured star beam quintessence
night after decadent night.

Once I even dropped down after you
into a world where the birds flew
in white flocks and the ships on the horizon
snapped mighty teeth, licking their lips
for a taste of the dirt on my shoes.

I found you there in your rain forest.
You served golden tea in china cups.

We layered mushrooms on your altar
that we picked off the roof of your cottage.

The land there loved me as much as you did.

Now here I sit awaiting that flash
that is your arrival to this hemisphere.
By now I know well the signs—
the eucalyptus breeze that licks at my earlobe,
the rumbling ground and the hole swept wider
with your witch's broom,
the air itself fusing into maze of mirror—

you walk through me
and come out the other side.

Side

The men brought the pole.
The women dug the hole.
Together they inserted and
opened wide for creation.
Slender hands hold ribbons
and color dances around
and around, weaves
patterns into the god's perfection.
Fingers touch the tapestry.
Skin to skin hot with magic
she makes a wish with a kiss.
Her mouth fills with bliss.
The woman by her side
stumbles over her beauty
entranced by the dance
of her experience.
Outside of what happens now
or then, beyond shoulders touching
ancient eyes balloon up and up
to touch the white flesh of the moon.

Moon

Full in Scorpio
and the bed made
for unmaking
the costume zipped
for unzipping
the panties slipped on
for slipping off
the thighs clenched
for unclenching.

She came then
red light bright
in night side time
and the fear
jumped into our faces
and the room melted
into her eyes
and she crept
into the golden
bled out her love
onto the morning
she bled out her love

into mouths open;

drinking
ourselves full
of her

we became.

Became

I was Her and still hold Her red glow in my center.
Nothing negates that, not even the fear that rises
up asking to be claimed now that the bars of the cage
have evaporated, the force field that held Her prisoner
hit with Her lightning tongue, fuse blown with our minds.

Nothing you can do can prevent Her coming
now that the door has opened
and the crimson veils have billowed in
to cover all of our faces with once secret whims
now exposed to the daylight,
now brought to the market square

where She appears naked in the middle of the street
admired, desired, loved and loving the people who smile
and strip down to nothing, lay down their clothes
for Her bare feet to walk upon
and follow Her into the newest day.

Day

After you danced for us and we kissed your delicious
belly and your lips let slip a slick of tongue,
and your pelvis opened, showing me how to open again,
we met with the children running around their toys
and sat together on your couch, staring into the glow
of each other's eyes for hours, for days even, and even now
as we sit here across the world, we look into each other
so deeply we

free
      form

           fall

                  in

                        love.

Love

Do not be afraid to love men, women, the
very young, the very old, animals, plants,
sudden acquaintances, lifelong friends,
your children, your parents, strangers,
yourself.

(Das Energi, Paul Williams)

Snake said to Hummingbird
I have this urge
to eat and be eaten
so primal I cannot help it
nor wish to.

Sometimes it feels quite chaotic
all this creation and destruction.
Is there ever a place to simply
be still?

Hummingbird hovered
moving in one place
over the morning glory
and sticking her bright beak
into the star showed him.

Urge and urge and urge
Always sex.
All goes onward and outward,
nothing collapses

And to die is different from what any one supposed,
and luckier.

Inspired, his mouth opened to receive
his tail and somewhere in the center
of infinity, the word for the dance, for the song,
the symbol some one etched on the door of the house—

Ouroboros.

About the Poet

Kala Joy lives in a yurt, is madly in love with her partner and grateful to Mother Earth for all the beauty everywhere.

She and her Beloved have co-created an erotic film company, the birth of which inspired this book. You can find more about the film company at http://www.houseofecstasy.com.

She has recently started posting to an online blog (http://kalasnowflower.wordpress.com/) which will feature random poems, updates on her book releases, as well as details on her *Performance Art Poetry-Ecstatic Rituals* which embrace a blend of poetry, dance, music, art and magic and are in themselves poems written on the page of the moment. Her intention in offering these performances and the poems themselves is to share her life long love of contemplation, nature and the words that express her ecstatic experience of living.

www.ingramcontent.com/pod-product-compliance
Lightning Source LLC
Chambersburg PA
CBHW060623030426
42337CB00018B/3166